Introducing Woodcuts

Introducing Woodcuts

Gerald Woods

B T Batsford Limited London

Watson-Guptill Publications New York

First published 1968
Library of Congress Catalog Card Number 68-15772

Printed and bound in Great Britain by
Jarrold & Sons Ltd, Norwich
for the Publishers
B T Batsford Limited
4 Fitzhardinge Street London W1 and
Watson-Guptill Publications
165 West 46th Street New York NY 10036

Contents

Acknowledgment 7

Introduction 9

Section 1

Collecting and selecting timber 11
Plankwood, Boxwood, Plywood,
Linoleum

Section 2

Drawing and cutting 14
Working with plankwood 14
Tools 16
Engraving on boxwood 17
Tools 17

Section 3

Printing by hand and press 19
Simple printing methods 21
Printing presses 23
Colour 23

Section 4

Group projects: art school 25
(a) Environmental studies 26
(b) Imagery derived from
photography 33
(c) Exaggeration of scale 38
(d) Three-dimensional
printmaking 40
Miscellaneous prints 44
Group projects: secondary school 54
(a) Heads 55
(b) Shakespeare series 58
(c) Children's prints 62

Section 5

Programming a print 69

Section 6

Materials 76
Suppliers in Great Britain 79
Suppliers in the U.S.A. 80

Acknowledgment

My thanks are due to the staff and
students of Watford College of
Technology, School of Art, for their help
and co-operation in the production of this
book. I am particularly indebted to my
friends, Philip Thompson and Alan
Kitching, for their help and advice. For
permission to reproduce prints made by
students at Watford, I would like to thank
A. J. B. Sutherland, M.A., Head of School.
The prints made by young students, under
the direction of Paul England, were
generously provided by the Peckham
Manor School, London.

GW   Richmond 1968

Photographs by Thomas Smith
Line drawings by Ron Sambrooks

The image is a principle of our knowledge.
It is that from which our intellectual
activity begins, not as a passing stimulus,
but as an enduring foundation.

St Thomas Aquinas

Introduction

This book is a visual record of the ways in
which woodcutting, or relief processes,
have been applied within a school of art,
and a secondary school programme, over
a period of approximately three months.

I have not provided a manual of
technique, but a rudimentary description of
technique is contained within the various
sections of the book. Woodcutting, for the
making of prints, is one of the oldest of the
programmed arts. It was a valid system of
communication in medieval times, and was
instrumental in the education of vision
throughout Europe.

Today, the medium is increasingly
popular in schools, as a means of free
expression, and as a means of
embodying artistic solutions. The word
woodcut here is used to describe
woodcuts, wood engravings, and linocuts.

10

Section 1

Collecting and selecting timber

Timbers are divided into two main types: softwoods and hardwoods. Softwoods (pines, firs, spruces) have needle-like leaves; their wood is resinous and easy to cut into with a gouge. Hardwoods (oak, beech, teak) have broad leaves and, because they are non-resinous, they are more difficult to cut. All freshly sawn timber contains a high percentage of moisture; because of its complex cellular nature, timber takes six months to season, although it is also seasoned in kilns over a period of four days.

Woodcutting is perhaps the most humble of all the printmaking processes. A search for discarded timber in country lanes, or in the back streets of a city, can provide the raw material for making a woodcut block. Timber found in this way has usually been deformed by climatic diversities and should be thoroughly cleaned with a wire brush and warm water. When the timber has dried, it can be treated with linseed oil which will soak into the surface and make it more receptive to the adherence of printing ink. Whilst a piece of deformed or erratically textured timber might provide an interesting starting-point for a print, timber can be bought in blocks of the correct height, with the surface smoothly finished for more accurate cutting.

Plankwood

This is the most common type of wood selected for woodcuts, and is cut parallel to the tree trunk. The printmaker usually

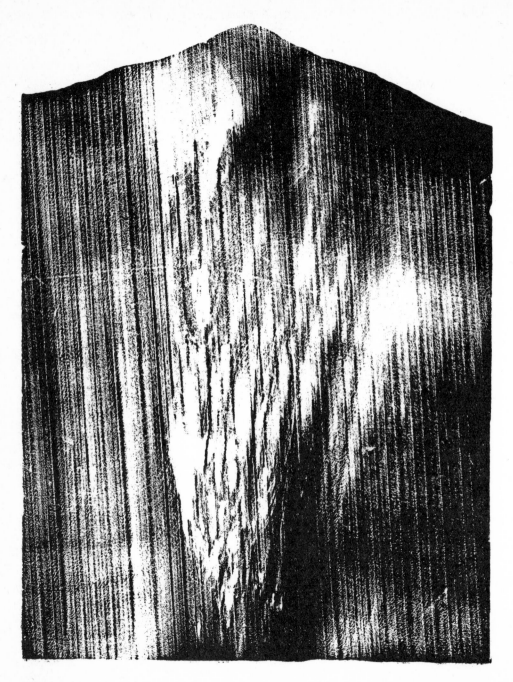

12

cuts in the direction of the grain, which runs the length of the plank and is often a decorative feature in itself; the pattern of the grain may, in fact, be considered as an integral part of the composition of a print. Prints taken from plankwood are recognisable by the strong character of the grain pattern.

Boxwood

Boxwood is the very hard wood used for wood engraving; it is cut at right angles to the length of the tree trunk. The surface of the wood is planed to a smooth finish so that the engraving tool can cut crisply through the surface of the block in any direction.

Plywood

Plywood is a man-made structural board of great strength, made from a number of thin sheets of wood glued together, with the grain of adjacent sheets at right angles to each other. For printing, it is only necessary to cut to the depth of the first layer of wood, which can actually be peeled away with the aid of a knife, wherever the artist wishes.

Linoleum
(the word linoleum is often shortened to lino)

Linoleum is one of the most popular and useful materials for relief printmaking; it is easily cut and stands up to a lot of hard wear during printing. It is ideal for large areas of colour and for free gestural strokes with gouges. Offcuts of lino can be purchased quite inexpensively from large department stores, and cut into sections for use in schools.

Section 2

Drawing and cutting
Working with plankwood

It is important to recognise the broad quality of line that is identifiable as an inherent mark of the medium, since any preconceived ideas of the completed work must surely be dictated by the nature and behaviour of the materials used.

For a detailed or fairly linear work, a hard wood such as pear or cherry is most suitable. The drawing can be made directly on to a sheet of tracing paper that has been trimmed to the size of the block. When the drawing is completed, the sheet of tracing paper is turned over, so that the drawing appears in reverse; it is then pasted on to the block, and when dry, the cutting can begin through the drawing into the surface of the block.

Most students prefer to draw directly on to the block without any concern for the reversal of the design, and for this purpose, a brush and ink, or a felt-tipped pen are most useful. An added wash of a middle tone makes the drawing appear very clearly, as the non-printing areas of the block are gradually cut away.

Before cutting begins, the artist must decide clearly whether he wants a white line drawing (a negative drawing) or a black line drawing, or a combination of both, remembering that the area of the block that is cut away is the non-printing area of the block. Some of these tonal problems can be tackled by making a preliminary drawing with pen and ink on the face of the block.

It is important to attain the correct posture and to ensure maximum comfort for cutting. If only for safety, the cutting hand should always be in front of the other hand, which is used to hold the block steady; the cutting hand should move *away* from the holding hand. For young students, a wooden bench-hook can be used to prevent the block from slipping. Most students ignore such aids, however, finding them obstructive to their creative action, and for their benefit, a supply of medical plasters or bandages should always be available!

Tools

There are three main types of cutting tool: V tools and gouges are gripped like a rod

The V tools are used to channel sharp lines, wide and narrow, according to the width of the V-shaped cutting edge of the tool. Gouges of varying widths render a softer, rounded line, since the cutting edge is more like a U; the larger gouges are mainly used for clearing away background areas of the block. The cutting knife is employed for preliminary cutting to define edges for scratching, or for scoring on the face of the block before using the other tools.

The knife is held as one might hold a pen or pencil, except that a tight grip is necessary to force the blade into the block, pulling the blade towards the body. V tools and gouges, are gripped like a rod in the palm of the hand, and the cutting action is directed *away* from the body.

All tools should be sharpened frequently at an angle where the cutting edge of the tool rests flatly on the sharpening stone. A carborundum wheel is rotated for the shaping of the cutting edge, but more generally, oil and slip-stones are used to *maintain* a fine edge to the tool. Rounded slip-stones are rubbed in the hollows of the gouges so that there is a uniformity in the sharpening procedure.

All of these tools cut readily through softwoods and lino. It is much easier to cut lino if it is warmed slightly. For harder wood, it may be necessary to use a wooden mallet to force the gouge through the surface of the block. Mistakes in cutting can sometimes be corrected by filling in an area, wrongly gouged away, with a mixture of plaster of paris and glue or plastic wood; the surface of the block should be sand-papered after filling.

Engraving on boxwood

It is possible to obtain a very fine degree of
accuracy on an end-grain boxwood block;
this is because of the well-finished hard
surface of the wood, through which the
engraving tool glides smoothly in any
direction. The logs from which the blocks
are cut are rarely more than 12 in. in
diameter; this means that an average size
for a block is 6 in. × 4 in., but larger blocks
are made by joining several smaller blocks
together. Blocks should be stored rather
like books on a shelf, as they are liable to
crack under any pressure during storage.

The drawing can be made directly on to
the face of the block, using a pen or pencil,
or a preliminary drawing on paper can be
traced down, using a carbon sheet. The
beginner is often tempted to use wood
engraving as a means of reproducing a
drawing in the precise terms of another
medium. It is a good idea, therefore, to
make trial cuts on an old block to discover
the variety of cutting patterns that can be
made with different types of engraving
tools; this will also help the beginner to
gain confidence in the use and handling of
the tools. A leather pouch filled with sand
supports the block for engraving; it also
enables the block to be turned freely when
one is engraving curved lines.

Tools

There are three main types of engraving
tool, with variations of each. The burin is
the tool most frequently used, and the
main drawing is cut with it before using
the other tools. In section, the tool is a
diamond shape. Lines of varying widths
can be made with a burin, according to the
depth of the tool as it is forced through
the surface of the block.

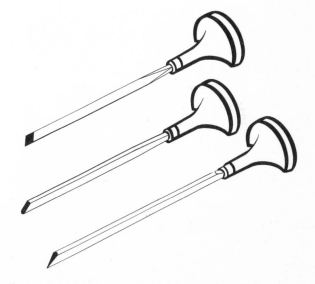

The scorper is the main clearing tool; it has a square, chisel-shaped edge which can also be used to make various textures on the block. Tint tools are used to make the tonal pattern on the block by engraving parallel lines which produce shades.

Other useful tools are the multiple tool and the spitstick. The multiple tool has several engraving tips, which can cut a series of thin parallel lines in one action, producing a shade or tint. The spitstick is particularly useful for cutting curved lines.

In the cutting of plankwood, the action of the tool and the arm in which it is held, are as one; but for engraving on boxwood, the shaft of the tool is controlled by the fingertips, using the thumb as a guide or stop against which the point of the engraving tool can slide into the surface of the block. The length of the shaft almost rests on the surface; if the angle of the tool is too steep, the sharp point of the tool will become buried in the block and may break.

Engraving tools must be in perfect condition for cutting into boxwood. The tip of the tool is sharpened on Arkansas stone, using a drop of machine oil. The shaft of the tool should be at an angle of about 45 degrees as the cutting edge is rubbed on the stone.

It is difficult to remedy any mistakes made during the engraving of a block. It can be done by removing the whole section of the block where the drawing has been fouled, and replacing the area with a fresh piece of boxwood; but this procedure calls for a great deal of precision, and should be done by a craftsman.

When ordering engraving tools from your dealer, it is a good idea to let him know the length of your hand, so that he can cut the shaft to a comfortable size for engraving.

Section 3
Printing by hand and press

A print can be taken from a block at any stage before the cutting is completed, even if only a few marks have been made. A black proof, taken in the early stages of cutting, can be useful in deciding on the tonal balance of the print before cutting away further parts of the block. The proofing of partially cut blocks is essentially a creative action, since decisions regarding composition and tonal qualities are made at this stage. It is a good idea to keep *all* the proofs, from the first print bearing a few white lines to the completed composition, so that the development of the print can be seen. Printing is the climax of the craft, and there is always a certain amount of anticipation as the first print is lifted from the block.

19

Simple printing methods

In secondary schools, there may be groups of thirty or forty young people cutting blocks at the same time, so that simple printing techniques are required to enable them all to take prints without having to wait in turn to use a press.

In the centre of the room, a large table covered in plate-glass, marble or hard plastic, could be the central inking area, so that each student can ink his block and return to his own work-bench to take a print from the block. The ink is laid in a thin line on the glass, using a palette knife, and the roller is moved over the line of ink, so that the rotation of the roller distributes an even film of ink on the glass before it is transferred from the roller to the block. The ink should be rolled evenly on to the block in several brisk movements.

When the block has been inked, a sheet of thin and fairly absorbent paper is laid carefully on the block, and two or three heavy weights are placed on top to keep the paper still. Using a spoon or any other suitably rounded object, the paper is burnished from the back by rubbing the spoon in circular movements. As one part of the paper is burnished, the weights are moved so that the other part can be burnished. Tonal variation can be obtained according to the amount of pressure exerted whilst burnishing. A corner of the print can be lifted from time to time to judge the effectiveness of the burnishing, and the print is lifted carefully from the block when the burnishing is completed.

For printing larger lino blocks without a press, the following method is quite effective: Place about a dozen sheets of newspaper on the floor, with the sheet of paper to be printed on top, the inked block is laid face downwards on the paper.

Pressure is applied by standing on top of the block with one foot, and stamping carefully with the other. Although quite a primitive method, the results can be quite surprising. Newsprint paper is quite suitable for all preliminary proofs, but for presentation prints a good quality drawing paper, which has been dampened slightly, should be used.

Printing presses

Direct pressure is required for printing a wood block. The simplest type of press producing this kind of pressure is the screw press that is used by bookbinders. The most popular press is the platen press; the blocks to be printed by a platen press are usually type height (0·918 in.), but the height of a thin block can be made up by using sheets of hardboard placed on the bed of the press underneath the block. For school use—particularly in secondary schools—the Minnesota Mining and Manufacturing Company, St Paul, Minnesota, U.S.A., has developed a compact, simplified press that works on the principle of the clothes wringer, passing the block between rollers.

In the printing of deformed or warped blocks, a soft packing should be placed on top of the printing paper, so that the printing paper is driven into the uneven surface of the block. In order to obtain a sharp image from an even block, a harder packing such as manilla board, or smooth card can be used.

When using printing rollers and inks, it is difficult to keep your hands clean, and inky marks may be transferred to the margins of the print, so it is advisable to handle the paper with folded strips of board sometimes called 'paper fingers'.

Colour

Each colour area of a print requires the cutting of a separate block. Thus, for a print in four colours, four separate blocks have to be cut.

Coloured inks may be either transparent or opaque. If transparent colours are used, consideration must be given to the effects of overprinting; if a blue is printed over a

yellow, it will make a green at the area where the colours overprint.

For wood engravings, a fairly stiff oil-based ink must be used; otherwise the fine lines would soon fill in.

Water-based inks are most suitable for large groups of young students as these water-soluble colours are less likely to damage clothing than oil-based inks; but the main advantage is that they dry very quickly, so that a four-colour print can be made in one day, whereas oil-based inks require about 10 to 12 hours drying time.

In order that the colours are printed in correct relation to one another, a registration sheet is required. The registration sheet illustrated is made with a sheet of thin board which must be larger than the printing paper. On this board must be fixed two sets of stops; one set for paper, and the other set for the block; the stops can be made of balsa wood or thick board. Each time a colour is printed, the paper and block are placed against the appropriate set of stops on the registration sheet.

The stages of a colour print may be summarised as follows:

1 Make a preliminary design in colour.
2 Trace the contours of each colour on tracing paper.
3 The tracing is turned over, and the first colour area is traced down on the first block.
4 Cut the first block and take a colour print, using the registration sheet.
5 Trace the colour on to the other blocks, one colour per block, cut each block, and print all the colours in register until the print is completed.
6 Amend colour scheme if necessary by varying ink colour and perhaps by further cutting to alter colour areas and overlaps of colour areas in printing.

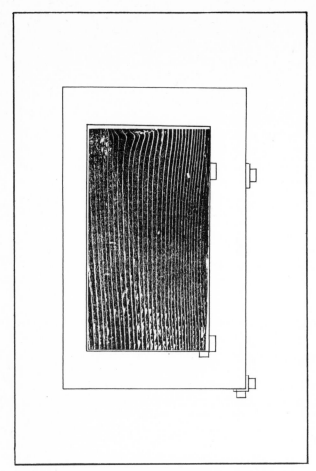
Registration on the platen press

Section 4

Group projects: art school

The artist teaching printmaking in a school of art today is faced with a number of problems. Whilst instructing students in the use of a particular technique, he must also ensure that the student's own initial freedom of expression is not destroyed by a total involvement with the technique itself. Every technique degenerates if it remains purely mechanical, that is, isolated from inspiration, but on the other hand, no idea can be fully conceived without a rule or discipline. The student must therefore be encouraged to give a great deal of preliminary thought to his work. The sole purpose of the medium that he selects should be a means of clarifying his ideas and statements, so that although the craft content is of secondary importance, a careful balance between idea and technique is maintained.

In many art schools, printmaking is taught by means of a series of projects; in the early stages the student is required to grasp and define the rudiments of a process by making experimental prints from found objects, and throughout the year the projects become more complex.

My own projects at Watford are usually designed as a means of solving specific problems exploring a variety of printmaking techniques. At the initial briefing, a sympathetic relationship is established by discussing fully the project and specifications. Students and teacher usually work as a team in the workshop.

The workshop is a kind of centre for graphic research and provides an ideal link between the painter and graphic designer.

Four projects are illustrated, with accompanying notes:
(a) Environmental studies
(b) Exaggeration of scale
(c) Imagery derived from photography
(d) Three-dimensional printmaking

(a) Environmental studies

This project was prepared for a small group of six second-year graphic design students. It was instigated by the re-building of the town centre at Watford and in particular the completion of a multi-storey car-park, which rises in a white concrete spiral from the centre of a group of office buildings.

At the initial briefing, we discussed the relationship of the human scale to the static shapes of the building. From a tonal point of view, it was particularly interesting; alternating with each white spiral of concrete wall is an equal area of concrete in dark shadow, being the recess between each floor. Each student was equipped with a camera when we visited the building, and we decided to record on film the combination of static and dynamic rhythms; one of the students was asked to run from the top of the building to the bottom, with the remaining students posted at various points taking photographs of him as he passed by, focusing on the moving figure or on the shapes of the building. The timing of this operation was all-important in order to get a good composition on film of the moving figure in relationship to the building. We were able to get proofs from the photographic film the same day; from these, each student selected a photograph which provided the information for a print,

(*a*)   General view of the car-park

to be made in any of the available print processes. The print I have chosen to illustrate this project was carried out in lino in three colours.

(*b*)   The photograph from which the print was derived

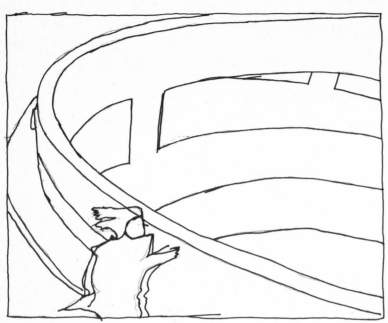

(*c*)   A free drawing from the photograph

(*d*)   Black proof of the first block

(*f*) Proof from the third block

(*e*) Proof from the second block

i) The main block is developed; the
distortion in this print was created by
cutting three circular areas within the
block, each section being rotated out of
register with the other sections

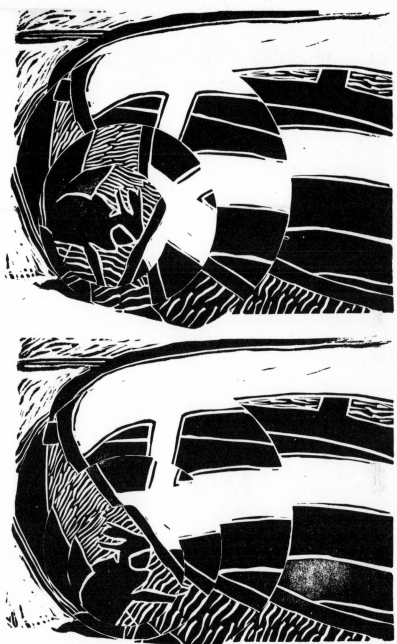

(b) Imagery derived from photography

The young generation of printmakers working today are very much inspired and impressed by the numerous photographic images that are churned out daily by various mass-media techniques, such as advertising, newspapers and television.

With the advent of such movements as 'pop art' the photographic image began to form an integral part of the composition in painting. In the field of printmaking, the hand craft techniques are now being combined with photo-mechanical processes which require special equipment and a knowledge of the various photographic techniques; in schools of art such techniques are made available to students. The prints I have chosen to illustrate this project, however, are *inspired* by photographs, rather than *using* photographs directly as a part of the printed composition.

(*a*) This print was inspired by a coarse-screen photograph seen in a daily newspaper. Very often, when an accident or disaster is reported in a newspaper, the accompanying photograph is dramatic and tense. The drawing was painted directly on to the block with a waterproof black drawing ink and it was cut and proofed in a black printing ink; but the black print seemed too heavy and not as dramatic as the half-tone photograph in the newspaper. The student had almost decided to abandon the block. But as a final experiment, he inked up the back of the lino block which is covered in a coarse cloth. If such a print had been taken from the back of a block that had not been cut, all that would have appeared would be the inked impression of the cloth; but because an image had been cut away on the block in question, there was considerable tonal change when the print was taken, the effect being similar to a half-tone photograph.

(*b, c, d*) This series of three prints are free interpretations of film-stills, cut and engraved on boxwood and pearwood.

(*b*)

(c)

(*d*)

(*e*) The technique for this print was discovered accidentally. A discarded printer's plate, containing a photographic image, was inked up with a hand roller; the student pressed his thumb on to the wet block and transferred the image on his thumb to a sheet of paper, so that a fragment of a photograph appeared within the shape of his thumb texture. This was continued (cleaning the thumb at each stage) until the composite picture was built up on paper. The quality of the print is reminiscent of a nineteenth-century line engraving.

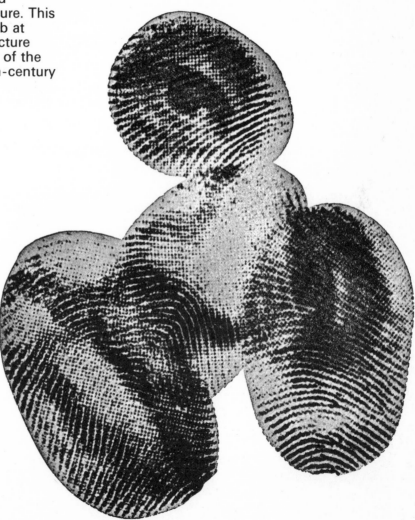

(c) Exaggeration of scale

Students were asked to turn out their pockets in a search for any interesting fragments of printed ephemera, such as a bus ticket or a discarded envelope. Alternatively, they were asked to select an everyday, mundane object, from which it would be possible to make an interesting, freely drawn interpretation of that object by adjusting the scale dramatically.

A choice of printmaking media was allowed, but paper sizes were specified as: minimum 20 in. × 25 in. and maximum 20 in. × 30 in. The main impact of this project is lost slightly in the accompanying illustration because of the necessary reduction to page size.

(*a*) Photograph of champagne cork

(*b*) Print derived from the object, printed on a sheet 20 in.×30 in. in four colours

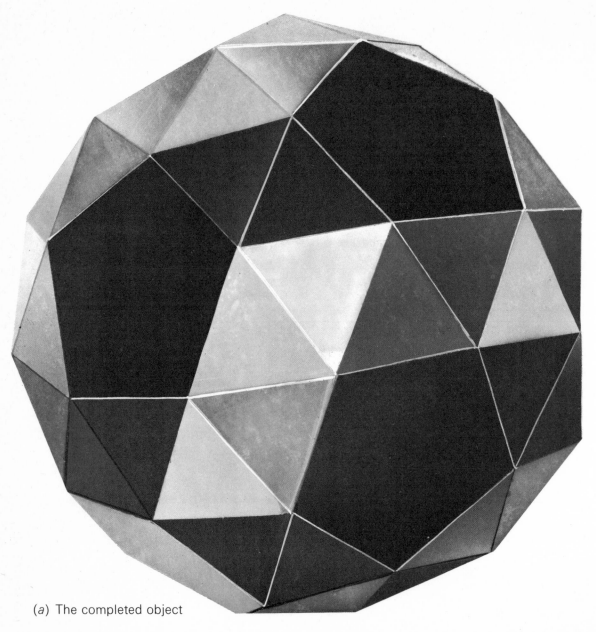

(*a*) The completed object

40

The idea for this print occurred to a student whilst she was attending a basic design lecture on modern building structure. One such structure was a complex of triangular patterns; the student believed that, with the use of colour, an interesting print could be made. She began by making a very accurate tracing of the original pattern and cut two colour blocks in lino, with the colours overprinting on some triangles to make a third colour. The finished print was very decorative, but she decided to carry it a stage further by cutting the printed area away from the paper, leaving flaps at the edge for pasting; by scoring along the appropriate sections of the print with a knife, the print was made up into a ball of triangles. This print demonstrates the possibility of using lino in precise terms.

(*b*) Print from the first block

(*c*) Print from the second block

(*d*) Blocks registered and printed in colour

The Car An embossed piece of metal
from an old fire screen was used as a
background block to this print

Miscellaneous prints

Although students are required to do a number of set projects throughout the year, they very often get ideas for prints from related fields of study in graphic design, colour and design, and history of art programmes. They may use printmaking as a vehicle for illustrating a particular book they have read, or as a means of making a drawing direct from a model. When a student has an idea for this kind of work, the teacher should discuss which print medium is most suitable for expressing that idea, and should generally follow the print through each stage, offering technical advice when necessary. At certain periods of the year, prints are pinned on the wall and a general criticism is given by the teacher and perhaps by one or two visiting printmakers.

The following prints are a miscellany collected from students' portfolios.

Portraits

Dream and Mirrors
A direct print from a
lino block

45

48

49

Moscow   Wooden veneers were used for
the background

51

This pattern was made with large pieces of wooden printing type; the word 'sun' is printed in three languages

Group projects : secondary school

In a school of art, an average group of students numbers about ten, but a secondary school teacher may have as many as thirty or forty students in one morning, and another group, equally large, in the afternoon. Print projects have to be well planned to cope with such numbers. The simple burnishing techniques already described should be possible and some of the more serious-minded students may attempt wood engraving and other more advanced colour techniques. Another point of comparison is that students at an art school presumably have a vocational interest in their work, whereas a large proportion of students in the art class of a secondary school may have little or no interest in art subjects.

Although allowances for materials in secondary schools are now quite generous, the teacher will find that stocks of lino will very quickly get used up, so that less expensive materials, such as hardboard and cardboard, may have to be used; but very often, students might enjoy searching for odd scraps of timber at home. The Minnesota Mining and Manufacturing Company, St Paul, Minnesota, U.S.A., has recently developed a 'printmaker's plate' similar to linoleum, but thin enough to cut with scissors, and adhesive backed for mounting. The product is intended primarily for schools.

In a number of secondary schools that I have visited students were simply given cutting tools and lino and told to make a print. Sometimes this non-project idea works quite well, since many younger students have a highly developed imaginative sense, which is lacking in older students at art schools.

Young students very often enjoy group activities. A large wall mural could be made by each student printing a section of that mural. Repeat patterns are also very popular. In the autumn term, linocutting usually becomes the main means of making Christmas cards.

The secondary school from which I collected prints was not specially selected for its reputation for graphic art; it was simply the first school that I visited. It was a pleasant surprise to find that the school had a graphic arts room where in addition to printmaking, students printed a school magazine and made motion pictures. The room was also equipped with a large platen press and a lithograph press. However, such elaborate facilities are rare in most secondary schools in Great Britain or in the United States.

(a) Heads

The only limitations imposed on the students for this project were that of size and that the print should be printed in black only. It is interesting to note that, in most cases, the heads occupy the whole area of the lino. Also note the way in which direct cutting of this kind reflects, in a very positive way, the character of each individual; one does not often see such forceful expression in the work of older students. It is in prints such as these that one is able to define the characteristic strength of the medium. There were many prints to select from and I have included as many as space will allow.

56

The students were asked to illustrate Shakespearian plays, that they had been reading in English literature classes, by

means of a black and white woodcut or linocut. The very rich tonal qualities of these prints remind one of the woodcuts that were made in Florence during the fifteenth century.

60

(c) Children's prints

I was recently asked to take over some rooms in an old children's school in Watford, which were required as extra accommodation for the school of art. A few weeks prior to my occupying the rooms, the children were moved to a new school in the suburbs. When I began to clear the cupboards, I discovered a large pile of lino blocks, some of which I printed and liked so much that I thought they should be included in this section.

Section 5

Programming a print

As the older presses become more difficult to find, more and more schools are investing in a modern cylinder proof press, and I believe it is worth while to mention a method of printmaking that is possible only with this type of press. With the other types of press mentioned a special registration sheet was necessary, and paper was laid on to the block by hand; but with the cylinder proof press paper is fed into grippers on the impression cylinder and comes into contact with the block as the cylinder is rotated by means of a handle at the side of the press. Paper is registered by an adjustable gauge attached to the press, which is much more precise than the sheet registration method. The movement of the block and the paper can be controlled separately, and by planning such movements, some interesting experiments can be made. The prints illustrating this section were made in the following way:

A single cut block was fixed on the bed of the press in a specified position (using the locking devices that are used for metal type). The paper was fed into the grippers and a print was taken, the block was then moved to the next planned position and the same paper bearing the first impression was printed again, so that gradually an abstract image is built up. By rotating the edge of the paper each time as it is fed into the press, the pattern becomes even more complex. The inking system on these presses is usually automatic, but sensitive features, such as the wide grain of a plankwood block, do not print very well. All the blocks used must be exactly type-height.

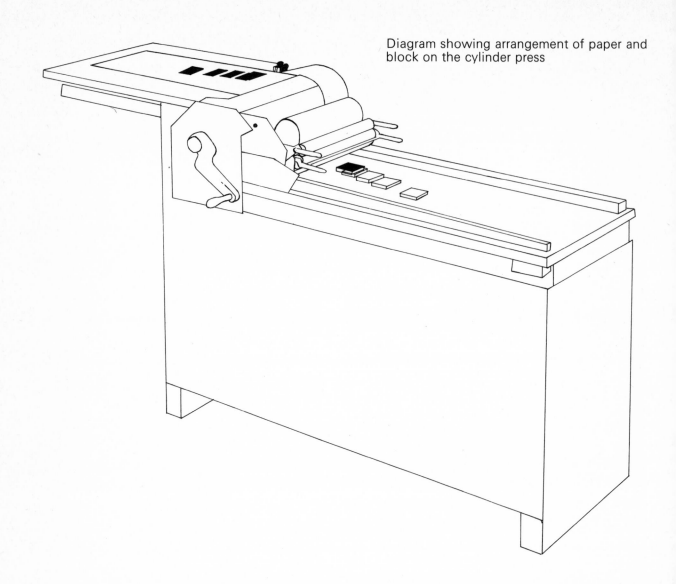

Diagram showing arrangement of paper and block on the cylinder press

Photograph of cylinder press

Prints made on the cylinder press

73

75

Section 6 Materials

Paper
Proofing

Newsprint is quite suitable for proofing woodcuts and wood engravings, but it deteriorates quite rapidly after a few months, so that it should not be used for finished prints.

Newsprint can be bought by the ream, the size of the sheet is usually 20 in.×30 in., or odd rolls of newsprint can be purchased at a modest price from a local newspaper printing works.

Brown wrapping paper and sugar (construction) paper are very good for proofing; in fact, any paper with a reasonably absorbent surface will do.

Presentation prints

For wood engravings, a paper with a smooth surface is essential; a coarse-grained paper would not show all the fine details of the block.

Basingwerk Parchment is recommended for engravings; it is an excellent paper and is no more expensive than ordinary drawing paper.

Woodcuts require a good quality white drawing paper; the tones of the print will be more intense if the paper is dampened slightly with a sponge.

Fine editions

Hosho 150 and Barcham Green Waterleaf are very fine Japanese and English hand-made papers; they are too expensive for general school use, but small quantities could be stocked for exhibition purposes.

Basic tools and other materials

Cutting knife
V tools, 3 sizes
Gouges, 3 sizes
Burin
Scorper
Spitstick
Multiple tool
Burnishing spoon
or press
Leather sandbag
Metal weights
Rollers
Ink slab
Palette knives
Pencil
Arkansas stone
Carborundum stone
Slip-stones
Oil can
Wire brush
Wood saw
Tracing paper
Carbon paper

Inks

Both water-based and oil-based inks can
be used for woodcuts and linocuts. The
oil-based inks are generally brighter and
preferable for overprinting techniques.
They are slower to dry, but a drying paste
can be added to the ink to speed up the
drying considerably. Tinting-medium,
mixed with the ink, makes it less stiff and
more transparent. Opaque white is added
for colour tints.

The ink is sold in tins and tubes; I have found that large tins tend to be more economical. It is better to buy inks from a well known manufacturer, since his inks will be made according to the high standards of the printing industry, so that they will be equally suitable for printmaking. It is worth while buying a good quality black ink, especially for wood engravings; some firms manufacture a stiff ink called woodcut black.

Water-based inks tend to be a little more opaque, but they can be reduced by adding tinting-medium. They are cleaner to handle, easier to wash off hands and clothing, and dry quickly. They are ideal for use in schools.

Oil paints and other substitutes can be used, but printing inks are not expensive.

Rollers

There are three main types of roller: composition rubber, plastic, and gelatine. I prefer the composition rubber rollers, but they need careful handling; if left near a window on a hot day, the rubber melts, or if the rubber is left in contact with a sharp surface, it will become deformed. It is a good idea to screw hooks to the ends of the roller handles so that they can be suspended vertically when not in use.

An average-sized roller is 6 in. wide and $1\frac{1}{2}$ in. in diameter, but several smaller rollers are also useful.

Suppliers in Great Britain

General

T. N. Lawrence & Son Ltd, 2—4 Bleeding
   Heart Yard, Greville Street, London E.C.1
This firm is one of the best known
suppliers. The small showroom, hidden
away in the city of London, contains a vast
selection of materials. I would recommend
in particular his tools and papers, as well
as rollers and boxwood blocks.

Basic tools, and presses for schools

Dryad Handicrafts, Northgates, Leicester
Dryads are specialist school suppliers; they
can provide all the materials necessary for
woodcuts, linocuts, and wood engravings.
They also produce an inexpensive press
for linocuts and woodcuts, as well as the
screw-type bookbinders' press.
Cylinder Press, Soldans Ltd, 23 Benwell
   Road, London N.7
Edwin Evans, 1 Salisbury Square, London
   E.C.4
Hewitt Brothers, 25 Field Street, London
   W.C.1

Suppliers in the U.S.A.

General

Graphic Chemical & Ink Co., P.O. Box 127,
    Villa Park, Illinois
J. Johnson & Co., 51 Manhasset Avenue,
    Manhasset, New York
Craftools Inc., 1 Industrial Road,
    Wood-Ridge, New Jersey
California Ink Co., 2939 East Pico,
    Boulevard, Los Angeles, California
Cronite Co. Inc., 35 Park Place, New York

Presses

Minnesota Mining & Manufacturing Co.,
    2501 Hudson Road, St Paul 19,
    Minnesota (also for plates)
Dickerson Combination Press, Util
    International Inc., 404 Broadway,
    Box 271, South Haven, Michigan

Fine paper

Andrews Nelson Whitehead, 7 Laight
    Street, New York 10013

Oriental paper

Japan Paper Co., 100 East 31st Street,
    New York 10016